GOD MOMENTS

30 reflections to start or end your day

Jennifer Rees Larcombe

MONARCH
B O O K S

Oxford, UK, and Grand Rapids, USA

Published by Monarch Books
an imprint of
Lion Hudson plc
Wilkinson House, Jordan Hill Road,
Oxford OX2 8DR, England
Email: monarch@lionhudson.com
www.lionhudson.com/monarch

ISBN 978 0 85721 693 9

First edition 2016

Acknowledgments
See page 93

A catalogue record for this book is available from the British Library

Printed and bound in Poland, December 2015, LH44

For Carol – with many thanks

Contents

1
Sea Anemones

When my children were young we spent our holidays by a rocky beach in Devon. One day when the tide was way out we were climbing over some boulders when my three-year-old shouted excitedly,

"Look! Someone's stuck lumps of red jelly on these rocks." Jelly was her favourite party food!

"Just wait until the tide comes in," I told her, "then those jelly lumps will open up into beautiful flowers."

Sometimes I find it hard to connect with God when I want to spend time with Him. Business, tricky relationships or fatigue may have closed my heart as tightly as those anemones above the tideline. So I give myself time to picture the flat-calm summer tide slowly lapping up the rock until I'm completely enveloped in the ocean of His loving presence. Then I "watch" myself uncurling all those waving tendrils to allow Him to fill me and feed me. Visual things like that help me so much!

In him we live and move and have our being.

Acts 17:28

When the tide comes in anemones are not only submerged in water, they are also filled with water. They really are just like jelly lumps, with no skeleton to support them. Inside they are nothing but an empty tube (the gastrovascular cavity). Yet when this tube is full of seawater, they can stand up straight and tall because the water inside them gives them strength and stability.

… experience for yourselves the love of Christ… that
you may be filled through all your being… and become
a body wholly filled and flooded with God Himself!

Ephesians 3:19, AMP

Lord, I love it that I can be in You and You in me
all at the same time – just like a sea anemone. In
my own strength I feel nothing but a spineless
lump of jelly, but filled with You I can stand tall.

2

Putting a Smile on the Face of God

It totally astonishes me how often the Bible tells us that we "delight" God Almighty.

He brought me out into a spacious place; he rescued me because he delighted in me.

Psalm 18:19

We often think about how God makes *us* feel, giving us all that joy, peace, and confidence, but wondering how we make *Him* feel seems rather odd.

If we have a distorted view of God (perhaps because of disapproving adults in our childhood) we might worry that we constantly make Him angry. The idea that He might feel delighted to be close to us probably feels strange. Yet we all know how much our emotions are affected by the people with whom we share our lives.

Does He enjoy my excitement when I discover the first snowdrops of the year? Does He laugh, too, as we watch that daring little mouse climbing up the bird table to steal nuts?

Does He also cry with joy as we watch the first baby blue tits flutter out of the nesting box?

Becoming that aware of God's emotions also has a downside. When I'm snappy with a colleague or spoil someone's day with my grumbling does the smile fade from His face? Does living close to me often make Him sad? How does He feel about my endless fears, self-pity, and lack of trust?

I once spent two months as a temporary nanny in a large country house. My charge was a spoilt only child of four. I tried to fill his life with fun, stories and games, but all he would do was grizzle and say he was bored. I knew I could make him so happy, if only he'd let me, but nothing I did ever pleased him. I guess I was too inexperienced to understand him, but I well remember how miserable living with him felt.

Let every detail in your lives – words, actions, whatever – be done in the name of the Master, Jesus, thanking God the Father every step of the way.

Colossians 3:17, THE MESSAGE

Lord, it is staggering that I can choose to delight you today – or to sadden you. Help me to make Your pleasure my first priority.

3
The Hamster Wheel

I couldn't possibly sleep when I stayed with my granddaughter because of her pet hamster called Frank. He was seriously hyperactive and ran all night on his squeaky wheel. At last I got up and shook Frank out of his wheel and into his cosy cotton-wool bed. Then I firmly removed the wheel.

I went back to bed thinking how much of my time I spend spinning on my own wheel of worry – my thoughts going round and round, just like Frank, and getting nowhere. "Lord, I've asked you to change me so many times; why don't you deal with me as I just dealt with Frank?"

Next morning my Bible passage for the day was 2 Corinthians 12. Verse 9 in *The Message* leaped out at me. "My strength comes into its own in your weakness."

Suddenly I realized that all the things I most hate about myself – shyness, fears, anxiety – were actually the very things which keep on pushing me into God. When I have to walk into a room full of strangers I ask Him to walk in front of me. When something worries or frightens me, I turn to Him because I feel powerless to handle the situation without Him. Had I been born

bouncing with confidence, courage, and self-reliance I would be able to handle my own life without having to turn to Him so often. I began to wonder if I needed to accept my weakness as His gift to me and learn to see it as my greatest strength? Thinking that we can control our own lives is probably the illusion that keeps more people from God than murder, theft, or adultery.

For when I am weak, then I am strong.

2 Corinthians 12:10

Please forgive me for the many times I thought You must have got something badly wrong when You made me. You had 500 million sperm to choose from the night my mother conceived me so You must have picked the one with the kind of temperament You wanted for me. Even if circumstances and other people have since damaged and crushed my spirit You can still use my emotional scars to bring me closer to You. Thank You that I am "fearfully and wonderfully made".

4
Leaning

What does it mean to "trust" in God? King David definitely knew how to do that. In Psalm 25:1–2 (AMP) he says, "Unto You, O Lord, do I bring my life. O my God, I trust, lean on, rely on, and *am* confident in You." I remember someone once saying, "The Lord loves a good 'leaner'." Perhaps that's what trusting is?

I once had a little statue that I kept by my prayer chair. It was a model of an open hand, and leaning up against it was the figure of a child. Although she was standing, the whole weight of her body and head was resting on the palm of that hand, and her face looked deeply contented.

One day a very frail looking lady came to see me. "I've got cancer," she said. "So I need God. Can you fix that?" I made a cup of tea and we began to talk. "I've never been to church in my life," she admitted, "but I've always had this feeling that God would be there for me if I needed Him." I tried to explain about Jesus and the cross but I realized she was so pumped full of morphine for her pain that she really wasn't able to follow anything I said – all she could do was gaze at my statue.

Passing it to her I said, "That's all you have to do, just lean all of yourself on to the God who loved you enough to die for you." She understood instantly, and a wonderful smile transformed her face.

I gave her the statue to keep and a few weeks later her daughter came to tell me she had died. Then she added, "She kept that little model you gave her on the locker in the hospice; she used to lie there, looking at it all day long."

Who is this coming up from the wilderness, leaning on her beloved?

Song of Songs 8:5, NKJV

Lord, all I want is to be a good "leaner".

5
Surviving the Impossible

Isn't it good when a familiar Bible passage suddenly takes on new, fresh meaning when you read it in a version you've not used before? That happened to me yesterday when I read 2 Corinthians 4:8–12 in the New Jerusalem Bible. Paul has just been saying that we can see and experience all the power and glory of God simply by looking into the face of Jesus (verse 6). As we "look" (that is, "connect ourselves") to Him, we not only

appreciate His power and glory, but we also absorb it into our lives. It is that power, in us, which makes it possible to survive all the horrors Paul is about to describe.

We are subjected to every kind of hardship, but never distressed; we see no way out but we never despair; we are pursued but never cut off; knocked down, but still have some life in us; always we carry with us in our body the death of Jesus so that the life of Jesus, too, may be visible in our body.

2 Corinthians 4:8–11, NJB

It is that supernatural kind of hope, strength, and confidence which impresses our neighbours and colleagues as they watch us go through "impossible" situations. They can plainly see "the life of Jesus… visible in our mortal flesh", and witnessing that is far more likely to bring them to faith than a sermon – or a healing miracle, which they can all too easily explain away!

It started when God said, "Light up the darkness!" and our lives filled up with light as we saw and understood God in the face of Christ, all bright and beautiful.

2 Corinthians 4:6, THE MESSAGE

Father I feel bewildered and confused by some of the things that are happening to me and to my family right now. Help me to keep focused on Jesus so that I act and react just as He would (Philippians 3:10).

6
The Secret Garden

The formidable lady who was leading the quiet day was a gardener. So I was not surprised when she began the day by saying, "I want you all to think of your lives as a garden. Is it neat, weed-free, with clipped edges and straight paths? Or are you a cottage garden, overflowing with heaps of flowers and summer fruit. Are you in a winter season, with empty, frozen beds, or can you see new things beginning to grow?"

Because I am a gardener too, I had begun to enjoy the day when I heard the leader say "Do you have a Secret Garden? Is there a part of yourself that you have walled up because you want to hide? Perhaps you feel that if people 'met' the real you they might be bored or disappointed? Or maybe you're ashamed of something?"

She definitely hit a nerve there, and other people were also looking uncomfortable. I began to wonder if we all had an area of shame we badly wanted to hide? Shame is different from guilt because it is not so much about what we have done as what we feel we are. Guilt leads us to confession and forgiveness but shame often envelops us as a result of the attitudes of other people in our past. Seeing ourselves through their eyes we grow up always feeling a failure, unlovable, or not good enough.

As I reflected I wondered if perhaps we manage to keep these areas of our "gardens" well hidden behind walls covered in pretty ivy and climbing roses. No one ever suspects that inside we are looking at mountains of stinging nettles and brambles.

Later in the day I found some comforting verses in Song of Songs. They suggested that, although I do hide parts of myself away from other people, Jesus my Bridegroom loves all of me, even the messy bits. He doesn't reserve His love for the day when I've hacked down the weeds, He wants to come into my Secret Garden just as it is and help me to clear it out.

You have captured my heart...
Your love delights me... You
are my private [secret] garden, my treasure, my bride, a
secluded spring, a hidden fountain.

Song of Songs 4:9,10,12, NLT

He wants me to respond with the following verse.

> *Let my beloved come into his garden and taste its*
> *choice fruits. (Song of Songs 4:16)*

7
The Languages of Intimacy

On the morning of my first communion my rather imposing grandfather took me into his study for what he called "a serious talk". As I stood before him, shaking, he said, "From now on, whenever you go to church, always take God a present. The Bible says, 'No one is to appear before [the Lord] empty-handed'" (Exodus 23:15).

I thought he was talking about my pocket money but he continued, "Before you leave home, think of something in the past week which God has done for you. Then arrive early. Sit quietly. Offer your gift of thanks" (Hebrews 13:15).

He was helping me to form a good habit, but how sad if I had thought thanking God was only necessary once a week!

Apparently there are five "languages" by which we communicate love. Giving gifts; spending quality time; words of affirmation; acts of service; and physical touch. The list applies to loving God as well as partners, so long as we add "obedience" (John 14:21).

I hear someone saying, "But we can't touch God physically!" No, but the Bible often talks of "God's hand, His face, and being

held by His arms". Perhaps He gives us the gift of imagination so that we can picture ourselves taking His hand, enjoying His smile, or "feeling" His arm around us as we lean against Him.

While we all have our own favourite "love language" for God, I think He wants each of us to use all of them. If we only use "acts of service" without organizing our diaries to make room for "quality time" with Him, we will serve Him in our own strength. Giving large gifts of money can easily lead some people to think they do not need to attempt the other expressions of love.

Perhaps giving Him gifts of thanks, privately under our breath, throughout the day, might be one of the most beautiful of all the ways of loving Him? That's easy on a good day, but even on the worst of bad days we can usually find one tiny thing for which to give Him thanks. We might pray, "Lord it's terrible that I crashed the car, but thank you that no one was hurt."

Always be cheerful: thank God no matter what happens. This is the way God wants you, who belong to Christ Jesus, to live.

1 Thessalonians 5:16–18, *The Message*

My Father, I know you don't expect me to thank you for the difficult and painful things themselves, but help me to remember it gives you particular delight when I manage to notice the positive things among the gloom of a bad day.

8
Prisoners of Hope

I'll never forget the day when I went to tea with some old friends. In the middle of their sitting room floor stood a huge cage containing an extended family of lively gerbils.

They also had a litter of teenage kittens whose only desire was to eat the gerbils. They swarmed over the cage, clawing at the bars and hissing furiously. The gerbils, however, took no notice at all but continued to climb, swing, and play on their toys without even looking at the kittens. They vested their hope of survival in the strength of those bars.

There is a verse in the Bible which always reminds me of that crazy tea party. "Return to your fortress, O prisoners of hope…" (Zechariah 9:12).

We can be imprisoned by such things as despair, bitterness, doubt, or addiction. Alternatively we can take up residence behind the protective castle walls formed from all the promises of God. They fill the Bible from cover to cover and, so far, He has never broken a single one!

Naturally we all want to live inside those solid walls of hope but perhaps we worry we won't manage to stay there? We need

to stop trying to work up enough faith, and simply concentrate on the Lord Himself.

The God of hope [who fills you] as you trust in him, so that you may overflow with hope by the power of the Holy Spirit.

Romans 15:13

Please, Lord of Hope, help me to live as freely and lightly as those gerbils, whatever kind of enemies are rattling my cage.

9
Mustard Seeds

Sometimes we can look at other people, and the wonderful gifts and ministries God has given them, and think, "I'm useless, there's nothing I can do for God." Recently I met someone who definitely felt like that after she and her husband retired from running a large Christian organization.

"Suddenly," she explained, "I wasn't able to serve the Lord in any way. My husband had become disabled and I was his full-time carer. Then, one day, when I was planting mustard seeds on our windowsill, I remembered what Jesus had said about them. Tiny though they are, they grow into big trees where the birds can safely shelter (see Matthew 13:31–32).

"Lord," she had whispered, "I can't sow seeds in huge fields any more, or see great harvests, but would You give me one mustard seed to plant for You each day?"

Her seeds were simple – an encouraging email to someone working abroad, a friendly card to a "prodigal" nephew, a note of appreciation to their local hospital, or just a smile in the post office. What a great life ambition – just to do one little thing a day to build hope in someone else.

Light-seeds are planted in the souls of God's people,
Joy-seeds are planted in good heart-soil.

Psalm 97:11, *THE MESSAGE*

> *Lord You tell us not to despise "the day of small things" (Zechariah 4:10), so please help me to realize that the size or importance of any job I do for You is irrelevant because achievement and success don't interest You. Help me to remember that what You look for, when I serve You, is whether I do the job, however little or large, as an act of worship to please You.*

10
Wild Beasts

I've just discovered something that I never realized before. Mark 1:13 tells us. "[Jesus] stayed in the wilderness forty days… and He was with the wild beasts" (AMP). Alone and unarmed, not many of us would have wanted to face them. Yet lions and jackals can sometimes feel far less threatening than our own personal worst fears, which may be losing our spouse, financial security, and mental or physical health.

The things we dread most can often turn up in our dreams disguised as mad bulls or a pack of wolves. We try to run away, but our legs seem paralyzed! In my mind the wild beasts that stalked Jesus in the wilderness equate with fears, so I found the next part of verse 13 extremely comforting: "… and the angels ministered to Him [continually]."

An angel also comforted Jesus in Gethsemane when He was abandoned by His friends and so afraid He sweated blood (see Luke 22:43–44). This reassures me that when our very worst fears become reality, heaven's power and comfort will surround us, just as they surrounded Jesus.

However, there was a time when Jesus deliberately *refused* the help of angels. As He hung there alone on the cross, in excruciating agony, He could have called on thousands of warriors to swarm from heaven and wipe out the entire human race in a moment, but He stayed alone on the cross because He loved us.

Perhaps the separation from heaven had been His greatest dread? So, because He faced His worst fear we will never ever have to go through ours without Him.

Thank You, Lord, that even in the darkest and most desolate place you will always be beside me. "Your right hand will hold me."
(Psalm 139:9–11)

11
Plugging Into God

I grew up in the days when Christians were taught that it was vital to have what was called "A Quiet Time" every day. We were sure that if we failed to read a chunk of the Bible and to plod through our "Prayer List" at the start of the day something very bad would happen before bedtime!

Although I am really glad that the habit of meeting with God every day has become part of my core existence, I can also see that becoming too rigid about it has sent me off on some bad guilt trips; and I can totally understand why so many shy away from what has been labelled "The Bondage of the Quiet Time". We humans seem to love crushing the joy out of sacraments which God intended for our enjoyment – and His!

When a personal daily appointment with God becomes a religious ritual, a way of gaining "Brownie points" – or worse still an insurance policy – then something is badly wrong. When you really love someone and they adore you in return spending time with them is never an "ought" or a "should".

Surely connecting with God is supposed to be fun, refreshing, and spontaneous and I'm sure it is variety that keeps all that alive. Sometimes I'm just too tired to pray, or to wade through an obscure Bible passage, so I just sit in His presence, holding my Bible as if I were holding His hand. At other times I find new worship songs on YouTube, or try out a different Bible translation online: anything to keep out of a rut!

For me, my electric fire defines what I mean by my "QT". As I push its plug into the socket beside my special prayer chair, all the electrical power of the National Grid flows through the flex to keep me warm. As I sit there with God I'm "plugging myself in" to Him in the same way, so that all His power, tenderness, wisdom, and peace can flow into me and flow out to others during the day ahead.

In the morning, Lord, you hear my voice; in the morning
I lay my requests before you and wait expectantly.

Psalm 5:3

Well Lord, we both know I don't find it easy to
stay "full of You" all day! But thank You that You
let me keep on coming back to "plug in" once
again.

12
The Open Hand

This morning I felt I could "see" a tightly clenched fist which someone wanted to thrust angrily in God's direction. As I prayed about it I thought, "No one who felt that way would be reading a book like this – or would they?" Perhaps when we feel disappointed and hurt by God, our reactions

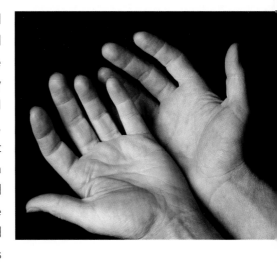

embarrass us because we want to be that "perfect Christ-like Christian". So we hide the unwelcome fist – so successfully that we even manage to forget it ourselves for long periods of time.

Then, a chance remark or line in a book forces the fist back to the surface and we feel we must hide it again – quickly. But must we? Suppose God wants us to face this area of pain and the grudge we are holding against Him? He knows that

the growth of our faith will be impeded unless we can find His healing.

I remember feeling that I was being slightly blasphemous when the idea of forgiving God first entered my head. I had been so sure that He would never allow the situation that I most dreaded to become a reality. Yet He had, and my resulting resentment was cutting me off from Him.

To forgive means to cease to blame, and I had indeed been blaming Him. Once I was able to release my feelings into His hands, and receive in exchange His peace, I felt I had been transformed.

Suppose God also wants you to uncurl your fist because He wants to place something unexpected in the palm of your hand? You may never have expected anything like it because you were so focused on what He had denied you. If you can accept what He is offering to you as His gift, then I believe it will bring you great delight.

When you [God] open your hand, they are satisfied with good things.

Psalm 104:28

Lord, I want to be free of all the areas in my life that I hold back from You. Please make me whole and filled with You throughout my entire being.

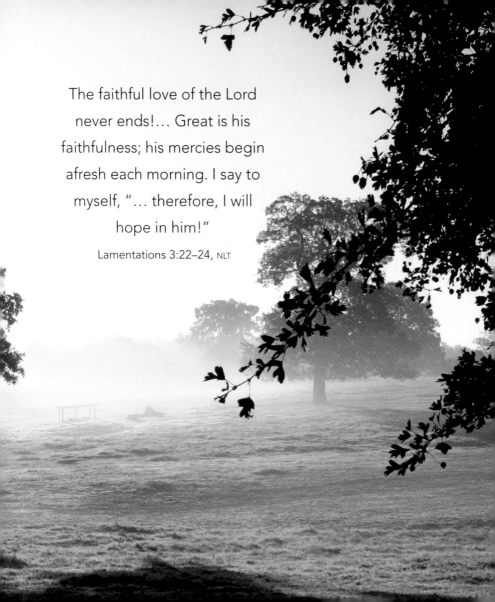

The faithful love of the Lord never ends!… Great is his faithfulness; his mercies begin afresh each morning. I say to myself, "… therefore, I will hope in him!"

Lamentations 3:22–24, NLT

13
Swallowing the Mystery

"Oh God, I just don't understand You!" Have you ever felt that kind of frustration rising inside you? I have!

The Lord explains so little, doesn't He? And also keeps us waiting for things so much longer than we feel He should! Someone told me she is going to give Him a clock when she gets to heaven! These days, when we are educated to the point where facts fall out of our ears and we can find out just about anything on Google, we find it hard to accept that God keeps so much of what He is doing a total mystery. I have a nasty suspicion this is because He knows our minds are too small to understand, and all He really needs us to do is trust Him.

Yesterday I was reading how God gave His people manna to eat for forty years as they roamed around in the desert. They must have puzzled endlessly about whether this food was "animal, vegetable or mineral?" Did it grow, or fall from the sky, and how could it possibly contain all the necessary nutrients to keep every age group fit and well? They called it manna ("What Is It?"). Because they realized they could not understand it:

they simply accepted it and swallowed down the mystery, day after day for forty years.

Perhaps we have to swallow our questions too, and leave God to explain – one day.

For as the sky soars high above earth, so the way I
work surpasses the way you work, and the way I think is
beyond the way you think.

Isaiah 55:9, THE MESSAGE

Lord I don't understand You, but I trust You!

14
Rejection

We don't all have good memories of our older brothers; James, Joseph, Simon, and Judas were four extremely fortunate little boys!

They adored their big brother. He kept them still as rocks for hours with His wonderful stories. Sometimes He would take them up into the hills and show them tiny creatures, bugs and birds, which no one else seemed to know were there. He had a way of making you feel safe when you were with Him and He always managed to see the funny side of things. When a day at school went badly wrong it was their big brother they went to, because He listened and comforted so well. When one of them grazed a knee or bumped their head His kindness soon took the pain away.

How could it have been possible for these four little boys to turn against that beloved brother when they grew up? Perhaps they felt He had ruined their lives the day He stood up in their local synagogue and announced He was the long-awaited Messiah? All their friends and neighbours were so furious they tried to kill Him, so the whole family were forced to move home

and business for their own safety. Then, rather than helping them build up their livelihood again, He was off round the country inflating His own ego with conjuring tricks.

"He's mentally ill," they told each other disgusted. "We'd better fetch him home and keep him locked up" (Mark 3:21, 31). "One thing's for sure," they agreed, "he certainly isn't the Messiah" (John 7:5).

Have you ever been misunderstood and rejected by your family, or by people you have worked with or worshipped beside? Jesus knows exactly how you feel because everything that He was, and all He had to give, was "rubbished" by the people who mattered most to Him. He utterly understands how you feel.

This isn't the neighbourhood bully mocking me – I
could take that… It's you! We grew up together!
You! My best friend! Those long hours of leisure
as we walked arm in arm, God a third party to our
conversation… Pile your troubles on God's shoulders –
He'll carry your load, He'll help you out.

Psalm 55:12–14, 22, THE MESSAGE

Lord, please help me to love my family as You
loved Yours.

15
Advertising

Yesterday morning, when I went to my local shops I was feeling down, tired, and grumpy. I am sure my face reflected my feelings. As I walked past the newsagent I saw the advert in the window for our church's next Alpha course and drove home hoping none of the people I plan to invite had seen me!

Jesus left us with a product to sell called Salvation (Mark 16:10). We advertise it by the way we live our normal lives and He wants us to stand out among our neighbours and colleagues like shining stars in a dark sky (see Philippians 2:15). We are the only "Jesus" they will ever meet and the only "Bible" they will ever read.

Jesus wants us to show other people that He is worth knowing and following because when we invite Him into our lives He fills them with His peace and supernatural joy. I'd known, as I had walked round the shops, that I could choose to take hold of that joy but instead I decided to stay crabby!

Joy isn't something synthetic we work up in public, but the gift Jesus left as our inheritance, the night before He died. "I have told you this so that my joy may be in you and that your joy may be complete" (John 15:11). An old friend left me some money to spend on my garden. Her executors transferred it into my bank account but it was no use to me until I chose to go to the bank with my bit of plastic and draw it out.

The ways of right-living people glow with light; the
longer they live, the brighter they shine.

Proverbs 4:18, *THE MESSAGE*

I read that verse this morning and thought, "Yes! It's easier to be full of joy when you're young, and life is going well. It feels harder when your arthritis is playing up and you keep losing the people you love! Yet surely it is then that the Jesus brand of joy shows up even more clearly?"

So sorry, Lord, that I am often such an old bag
full of grumbles and moans! Help me choose to
be full of Your joy – so people will want to "buy
into" the product You are offering them.

16
Distant Perspective

Early this spring I was struggling with some difficult situations in my life and knew I would have to make big decisions. My father always used to say, "When life gets confusing and you can't find a way through your problems, go where you can see far into the distance and you'll soon see your life in its proper perspective again."

My daughter's family have a log cabin set high on a cliff above the sea on one of the Gulf Islands in Canada. So when my son-in-law rang to ask if I would like to join them there for their spring break, I gave him an instant "Yes!"

Two days later I was on the plane, picturing myself sitting on the cabin veranda, gazing over the sea at forest-encrusted hills and distant snow-capped mountains…

For days I paced the cabin: it was too wet to go out and a thick grey "Vancouver Fog" enveloped us. So much for the therapeutic effect of distant views!

One evening, cuddled in a rug, I read this: "I will lift up my eyes to the hills. From whence comes my help? My help *comes* from the Lord, who made heaven and earth" (Psalm 121:1–2, NKJV).

"Well Lord," I told Him, "that's why I came all this way – to look towards those mountains so I can get my life at home back into proportion again." Then I saw the margin note beside the verses. "Pagans worshipped their idols on top of the hills, so they looked towards those 'high places' when they were in need of help. The psalmist reminds us that it is in Jehovah alone, not in places or people, that we find our help."

I could not see the snow-capped mountains but I knew for sure they were there behind the fog. I couldn't see God either, but I was just as certain He was there in the cabin with me.

Lord, I'm sorry I was so slow to see that it is YOU who will help me see my life in proportion. I didn't need human advice, counselling, or a holiday in the wilds. You will guide me through decisions and future changes, step by step.

17
Catching His Eye

Before I was married I was painfully shy and hated parties or crowds of strangers. After I met Tony, however, I was so much in love I soon found I could manage such occasions. Even if he was not right beside me we could still catch each other's eye through the swarm of heads with that secret look of "connection" and understanding. We shared smiles of private amusement or the silent signal, "It's definitely time to go!"

When I no longer had a husband to go with me to such events, I began to cultivate the habit of realizing that Jesus

came with me instead by deliberately "looking" into His face. I know from the Bible that He is watching me (2 Chronicles 16:9), sharing my thoughts (Psalm 139:1–2), and He even enjoys my sense of humour.

Those who look to him for help will be radiant with joy;
no shadow of shame will darken their faces.

Psalm 34:5, NLT

I once stayed in the home of two elderly sisters. They were putting me up because I was speaking at a mini conference in their church over the weekend. They were extremely kind-hearted but so unused to visitors that they nearly drove me mad with their incessant fussing. They never left me alone and talked continuously. Desperate for space to prepare my next

talk I told them I needed a walk round the block. "Oh but it's so cold, dear… here's my scarf… suppose you are attacked near that awful pub… whatever will you wear on your feet?"

Exasperated, I rolled my eyes to the ceiling and had the oddest feeling I could see Jesus. He was smiling at them affectionately as He raised his shoulders in a gentle shrug as much as to say, "But aren't they lovely?" Ever since then I've often looked up over someone's shoulder in the middle of a conversation and tried to gauge the expression I might expect to see on His face if only I could see it. I may be feeling intimidated, bored, and hurt by what the person is saying to me, but it is His attitude to them, which must determine mine.

My heart says of you, "Seek his face!" Your face, Lord, I will seek. (Psalm 27:8)

18
Praying Up, Not Down

When I first found this little phrase in an old book written 150 years ago, I didn't realize how much it would affect my prayer life. "Don't pray up, pray down!" As I pondered on it I realized that when I prayed I saw myself as a tiny ant on earth, yelling up at God above the great blue yonder, desperately trying to make Him change His mind over the people or situation which concerned me.

That is "Praying Up". So what is "Praying Down"?

The missionary teacher back in the 1880s had obviously got the idea from reading Ephesians 2:6 which tells us we are "seated with him [Christ] in the heavenly realms". The word "seated" is in the present tense – not "will be seated one day in eternity" but seated right now, *today*.

To accept the truth of that seems like an outrageous presumption, but we are there beside Him because of who we are. Kate Middleton was just an ordinary student, known only to her family and friends, but because she married a future king she became one of the best-known celebrities in the world with the right to sit beside her prince at state occasions. Similarly, we are joined to Christ, because we chose Him and He chose us, so we too, have the right to sit with Him.

Because we are looking down on the world from His angle and perspective "Praying Down" is all about sitting so close to Jesus that we discover *how* He wants us to pray. Then we simply ask Him to drop down good things on the people we point out to Him.

He [God] raised Christ from the dead and seated him at his right hand in the heavenly realms.

Ephesians 1:20

And God raised us up with Christ and seated us with him in the heavenly realms in Christ Jesus.

Ephesians 2:6

Jesus, this is just too big for my head! I'm just not worthy to sit up there beside You; and of course I'm not worthy! It was only because of what You did for me on the cross that made any of this possible. Thank You!

19
Off the Hook

Once I was asked to visit a girl who had been ill for the previous ten years. She lay in a darkened room because light and noise were intolerable to her. Various hospitals had done their best to find a cure for the illness that had robbed her of youth, but there seemed to be nothing they could do.

"I asked you to come," she said from under the duvet, "because I hear you believe in divine healing." I said that I did, but went on to explain that I felt God worked most easily when we ask Him into the centre of our lives so He can heal from the inside out. Then I added, "Have you ever asked Him in like that?"

"Oh no!" she said pushing aside the duvet and glaring at me. "I just want Him to heal me, I don't want Him in my heart!"

"Why's that?" I asked gently.

"Because if I did He would make me forgive my father, and I couldn't possibly do that!"

As she began to describe some of the things she had been put through as a child, fury filled me. In the end I had to interrupt. "It would be humanly impossible to forgive things like that!"

She looked at me. "But, surely you believe that if you don't forgive you can't be forgiven, and if you're not forgiven you can't have God in your heart? So why say it's impossible?"

"I said 'humanly impossible'," I replied. "Terrible things like these can only be forgiven when we are willing to let God forgive with us and through us."

"That would be like saying none of those awful things mattered," she snapped.

"They mattered all right!" I agreed. "And forgiveness means admitting that they mattered but choosing to forgive anyway."

"If I do that," she replied, pulling the covers back over her face, "I'll be letting my dad off the hook, and I want him there – permanently!"

She has remained unwell ever since and sadly *she* is the one who is stuck on the hook.

For if you forgive people… their reckless and wilful
sins, leaving them, letting them go, and giving up
resentment, your heavenly Father will also forgive you.
But if you do not forgive others… neither will your
Father forgive you…

Matthew 6:14–15, AMP

> *Lord, you put such a very high priority on*
> *forgiveness, so please show me if there is anyone*
> *I need to forgive.*

20
Castles of Can'ts

My five-year-old grandson was having a "castle craze" when he came to stay. I trudged him round Hever, Bodiam, and Pevensey, then he built his own version out of sheets, tables, and chairs, insisting on sleeping and eating inside it.

If anyone approached, other than me carrying food, he would chant, "I'm the King of the Castle, get down you Dirty Rascal!"

He made me think of how easily we all build ourselves castles. The stones we use for the walls are our "Can'ts". "I can't do this… I can't do that…" We feel safe behind our tightly closed drawbridges but they actually prevent us from "riding out" like a brave knight in armour to be the person God intended us to be. When we convince ourselves that if we never try new things there is no risk of failure we are forgetting Philippians 4:13: "I can do all things through Christ who strengthens me" (NKJV).

The apostle Paul knew a lot about castles, he was imprisoned in so many! Here is what he says about the self-protective castles we build for ourselves: "We are human, but we don't wage war as humans do. We use God's mighty weapons, not worldly weapons, to knock down the strongholds of human reasoning and to destroy false arguments" (2 Corinthians 10:3–4, NLT).

If you have discovered you are walled up behind too many "Can'ts" perhaps you could rewrite my grandson's jingle and use it whenever a negative thought creeps up behind you? "Jesus is the King of my Castle, get down you Dirty Rascal."

I can make it through anything in the One who makes me who I am.

Philippians 4:13, THE MESSAGE

Lord, I don't ask you for more self-confidence; but I do so badly need more God-confidence.

21
More Room for God

On a hot sultry summer day I went to hear the famous speaker Bill Johnson. The church was crammed with enthusiastic conference addicts when the air conditioning went off duty. By the afternoon session the heat was sending me to sleep. Suddenly I heard the words, "We can have as much of God in our lives as we want, but the amount we want can be measured by how much we are willing to move out in order to make room for Him." I was awake instantly; Bill's words had stirred a memory from the past.

When we were first married we lived in a delightful cottage by the green in a picturesque Hertfordshire village. As part of a church "outreach" programme we were asked to host a coffee and dessert evening in our home. A local Christian doctor would be invited to come and talk on "My faith and my job". We made a list of who we wanted to invite and then realized our tiny cottage would never hold that many. "Probably no one will want to come," we thought, but when all our neighbours answered their invitations with a "yes" we panicked.

Fortunately the weather that evening was fine, so out went sofa, armchairs, dinning table and sideboard, into the backyard. Then we borrowed cushions from everyone we knew and sat our guests on the floor and on every step of the stairs.

It was one of those evenings when the presence of God just seemed to hover over the whole house, impacting everyone there.

Somehow that memory seemed to illustrate for me exactly what Bill had been saying.

... let us strip off every weight that slows us down, especially the sin that so easily trips us up. And let us run with endurance the race God has set before us. We do this by keeping our eyes on Jesus, the champion who initiates and perfects our faith.

Hebrews 12:1–2, NLT

O Lord, there is so much clutter in the "house" of my life: things like the armchairs that are too comfortable to live without, self-indulgent habits, small dishonesties, unhelpful relationships or activities. Or the rigid, formal things like the dining table, the "oughts" and "shoulds" of Christian life, which become dead rituals, done because I can never say no! Please help me to clear out everything that prevents me from being full of You.

22
The Lucky Ones

I try hard not to envy people who seem to sail through life without any trauma, while for years I have lurched from one disaster to the next! I often meet other people who feel like this as well, "Why do some people get far more than their fair share of troubles?" they lament.

I first met Jane in hospital where she was facing major surgery. She told me she had suffered most of her life from bipolar disorder, which regularly plunged her into terrible periods of deep depression. She had also had to contend with a bewildering series of family tragedies. I asked her if she ever felt she had been unfairly treated in comparison to the lucky ones with easy lives. She thought for several minutes before answering. "Actually," she replied at last, "I think I'm the lucky one. You see I've always longed to know God intimately, not just academically, and I've come to realize that when your need of Him is paramount, that's when you really know Him.

"It's like poor old Job who, after going through all his suffering, admitted that he'd only ever known *about* God before, but now he knew him personally, like a friend" (Job 42:5).

As I watched the way Jane's face shone when she showed me her favourite psalms, I could see just how very blessed her life had been.

Yet I am always with you; you hold me by my right hand… Whom have I in heaven but you? And earth has nothing I desire besides you.

Psalm 73:23, 25

*If God hadn't been there for me, I never would have
made it. The minute I said, "I'm slipping, I'm falling,"
your love, God, took hold and held me fast. When I was
upset and beside myself, you calmed me down and
cheered me up.*

Psalm 94:17–19, THE MESSAGE

"Perhaps," finished Jane, "Those 'lucky' ones, with plain-
sailing lives, worry sometimes about how they would cope
when troubles come, because they've never had the chance to
find out how close the Lord comes at times like that."

*Lord, thank You that it is only when I discover
that You are close beside me in the darkest of
valleys that I appreciate how utterly safe I really
am (Psalm 23:4).*

23
The Clock Mender

My grandpa collected old clocks. When I stayed with him, the orchestra of chimes made sleep impossible! "Pop" loved taking them apart to clean every screw and cog because even a tiny speck of grease or dirt can slow a clock, or even stop it completely. He would become so absorbed in examining every tiny part of the machinery that he would screw up his eyes into slits.

I was reminded of him today when I read Psalm 11:4 in the New Living Translation: "The Lord still rules from heaven. He watches everyone closely, examining every person on earth." Apparently, when translated, the original Hebrew word "examine" means "screwing up your eyes to look at something very closely".

I feel safe when I think of God sitting in heaven looking down over the vast sweep of all humanity; but I like it even more that He also holds us close enough to see every detail of our lives, because He cares for each of us so intensely.

From heaven the Lord
looks down and sees
all mankind… the eyes
of the Lord are on
those who fear him…
We wait in hope for
the Lord: he is our
help and our shield.

Psalm 33:13, 18, 20

Lord, the English word,
"examine" sounds a bit
ominous. Yet I do want
You to look deeply into
my innermost being and
find those little specks of
dust and grit that stop
me from using well Your
gift of time.

24
God's Anticipatory Love

Writing books is often a lonely job, unlike speaking when you see people reacting to what you're saying. When you write you have no idea if your words will ever be read. Yet books can reach far more people than sermons ever can. As Henry David Thoreau wrote: "How many a man has dated a new era in his life from the reading of a book."

I had been praying for my neighbour for a long time before I dared to give her one of my books as a Christmas present. She said thank you politely, but later told me "it looked a bit too religious", so she shoved it unopened into a cupboard. She refused my invitations to guest services or Alpha introduction evenings and when I moved away I have to confess I stopped praying for her.

Years later, after her husband had left her, she was clearing out all her possessions and found the book. That night she read it from cover to cover, and met God for the first time. She discovered my address via a mutual friend and wrote: "All those years ago, God must have known the exact right time when I'd need that book."

Cast your bread upon the waters, for you will find it after many days.

Ecclesiastes 11:1, NKJV

Lord, I love Your anticipatory love! You so often get things ready for us long before we discover we need them. Help me remember that when I make You Lord of my present moment, it allows You to be Lord of my past and my future as well.

25
Timelessness

"But more than all… there is a time for timelessness."

This quote by the twentieth-century poet E. E. Cummings started me thinking when a friend emailed it to me recently. At first I laughed, "That might have been true a hundred years ago, but every five minutes counts these days." We have to dash through our tightly scheduled days texting as we run! For Christians, even Sundays are rigidly timetabled by church activities. When I plan a quiet day away with God I still take a "to-do list" in case I "waste time". I'm sick of this rush!

God designed us to work at our peak only if we take one day of complete rest once a week. I guess that would be impossible for most of us, but to avoid burnout I'm going to go through my diary and put TD beside an occasional date and make them Timeless Days when I don't allow myself to plan anything but just wait and see what I feel like doing on the day. I dare you to do the same!

Be still and know that I am God.

Psalm 46:10

Lord, please teach me how to "waste time" in Your presence.

26
Jesus Be the Centre

Recently, I woke dreading the day ahead. There were just too many things to do and difficult people to handle. I even felt too tired and scared to get dressed – let alone walk through the day.

Have you ever had the tune and words of a song drop into your head like an email appearing in your inbox? That is exactly what happened to me as I brushed my teeth that morning. "Jesus, be the centre… Be the wind in these sails, be the reason that I live…" As I dashed towards the cereal packet I remembered a picture my granny used to have on the wall of her sitting room. It was probably only a cheap print of some famous oil painting but as a child I loved it. It showed a massive sailing ship, with three masts and at least forty-six sails bulging with the power of a vigorous tailwind. It cut through a rough sea with silent dignity.

I kept the song and the picture in my heart all day and whenever I sagged or felt overwhelmed I hummed the tune to myself. As I went to bed that night I realized I actually felt far less tired than I had when I got up in the morning!

Again Jesus said, "Peace be with you! As the Father has sent me, I am sending you." And with that he breathed on them and said, "Receive the Holy Spirit."

John 20:21–22

Thank You, Jesus, for the power of Your Holy Spirit, which has blown me through the rough seas of today.

27
God's Wonderful "Forgettery"

The day after I'd had that wonderful experience of being "blown through the day by the Spirit", everything seemed to go wrong. I began the morning by writing about the picture and the song in my journal and I was so sure that I would live through this new day just as triumphantly.

Oh dear! I totally messed up! Instead of Jesus being the centre I allowed a very grumpy me to take his place. I could see my bad mood and snappy remarks wiping the joy out of other people's faces and I hated myself for it!

By the end of the day, I felt as if that wonderful sailing ship had arrived back in the harbour with snapped masts and shredded sails. When I went to bed, all I felt I deserved to read was Lamentations! However, by chapter 3 I was feeling considerably better.

… My soul is downcast within me. Yet this I call to mind and therefore I have hope: Because of the Lord's great love we are not consumed, for his compassions never fail. They are new every morning; great is your

faithfulness. I say to myself, "The Lord is my portion;
therefore I will wait for him." The Lord is good to those
whose hope is in him, to the one who seeks him.

Lamentations 3:20–25

Fortunately for us the Lord does not require us to be perfect,
just to repent often! By the time I had said sorry for the things I
regretted that day, He had totally forgotten them!

Lord, I do so love Your "Forgettery"!

28
Willing to Fit In

I came precariously close to murder once! My peaceful, happy life had just been bombed into ruins. Then a well-meaning, but extremely irritating, friend patted my arm and said, "Never mind, dearie, just remember 'God works all things together for good.'"

I think this is the most infuriating verse in the Bible – here it is in full. "And we know that in all things God works for the good of those who love him, who have been called according to his purpose" (Romans 8:28). What makes it even more maddening is that it happens to be *true!* But of course you never realize that until much later.

I looked at my friend with loathing. I didn't want to be "called according to God's purpose"; I just wanted my old life back! Neither could I see how anything "good" could possibly come out of so much destruction and desolation.

Looking back now, of course, I can clearly see the wonderful plans God really did have for me, and my whole family, through that disaster, but I'm embarrassed now to think how furiously I argued with Him at the time!

Perhaps the "good" that God was planning could never have happened until I stopped arguing and realized I needed to be willing to "be called according to his purpose," that is, to fit in with His plans rather than demanding that He fitted in with mine.

It was a very decisive moment for me when, in the middle of raging and swearing at Him one day, I suddenly felt surrounded by His presence and love. I felt Him say, "Let me into the centre of all the pain you are carrying in your heart – so I can help you." Knowing His love and presence right at the core of my life made it possible for me to be willing to go along with whatever His purposes might be.

Perhaps to "love God" means to trust Him enough to let Him do things His way?

Lord, I'm so sorry for all the times when I've thought, "You really got it wrong this time!" Help me to remember that love and trust go together like the two wings on a bird.

29
Woodlice

Most of us don't like change! Yet change is inevitable, as a wise man once said, "To live is to grow; to grow is to change; so to live successfully means to change often." Life forces us to change from being a baby to a schoolchild, a wage earner to a senior citizen – with countless other new identities in between! God longs to use these outward upheavals to transform us inwardly, making us more like Jesus.

Even good changes we plan ourselves can involve loss of some kind, and most of us feel extremely vulnerable stuck in the gap between the person we used to be and one we haven't yet become!

I was thinking about all that as I walked out to my woodpile to fetch a log for the fire. Lifting it sent a clutch of woodlice scurrying in all directions. Like us woodlice have to change in order to grow. They have no skeletons; it is the hard, protective carapace that holds them together. The only way they grow is to shed that outer layer and then wait for new skin to harden. During that "gap" they are extremely vulnerable to predators – and, similarly, so are we!

Some Christians do not survive major change. They are attacked by doubts about God's love and power, and by fears and resentments. Others develop a new, hard skin of faith as they allow God to reinvent them.

Perhaps we need to remember, when we or our friends hit times of change, that the "waiting gap" can make us feel very fragile – and it always takes longer than we think it should! Yet through it God can grow us into the bigger person He always planned for us to be!

You will be called by a new name. A name given by the Lord himself… Your new name will be "God Is Pleased with Her".

Isaiah 62:2, 4 GNB

Jesus, You are changing me,
By Your Spirit You are making me like You.
Jesus, You're transforming me,
That Your loveliness may be seen in all I do.
You are the potter and I am the clay,
Help me to be willing to let You have Your way.

Marilyn Baker

30
Standing in His Presence

I've discovered something else very releasing about prayer recently. Sometimes I feel a bit overwhelmed when it comes to praying for my large family and close friends – by the end of a long life you have collected so many people you genuinely want to pray for each day, but saying all their names over to God every day takes so long!

I passionately believe in the power of prayer, so it was a huge relief to me when I discovered something a few months back. I was reading Exodus 28, which is full of God's design for the robes of His High Priest. On the breast panel two huge gemstones were set into gold filigree. Engraved on the jewels were the names of the twelve sons of Jacob. "In this way, Aaron will carry the names of the tribes of Israel on the sacred chestpiece over his heart when he goes into the Holy Place. This will be a continual reminder that he represents the people when he comes before the Lord" (Exodus 28:29 NLT).

That little verse has revolutionized the way I pray for the people I love. I think of myself as their representative, standing before the throne of God. I am holding them, resting on my heart, as I expose them to the laser light beam of His presence and love. Some of those friends have wandered a long way from Him, while others serve Him with all their energy, but He knows each one of them intimately and I can leave Him to do exactly what is best for them.

> *Lord I am bringing You the names of the people I love, and like those High Priests of long ago I say: "May the Lord bless you and protect you. May the Lord smile on you and be gracious to you. May the Lord show you his favour and give you his peace." (Numbers 6:24–26, NLT)*

Jennifer Rees Larcombe runs "Beauty from Ashes" from her home in the heart of the Kent countryside. It is a safe place where people who are hurting come for peace, space and to receive prayer. Jennifer also runs healing days, retreats, quiet days, and conferences.

Website: www.beautyfromashes.co.uk

Contact us on: office@beautyfromashes.co.uk

www.facebook.com/beautyfromashes/JRL

Also available from Jennifer Rees Larcombe:

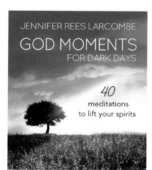

Jen Rees Larcombe knows from her own life how tough things can get. Here are 40 short meditations for dark days, each with an honest, straightforward prayer. Beautifully illustrated, it will make a welcome companion and a heart-warming gift.

978-0-85721-694-6

www.lionhudson.com

Acknowledgments

Extract p. 77 taken from "since feeling is first". Copyright 1926, 1954, © 1991 by the Trustees for the E. E. Cummings Trust. Copyright © 1985 by George James Firmage, from Complete Poems: 1904–1962 by E. E. Cummings, edited by George J. Firmage. Used by permission of Liveright Publishing Corporation.

Extract p. 79 taken from "Be the Centre" by Michael Frye © 1999 Vineyard Songs UK (Adm Song Solutions www.songsolutions. org). All rights reserved. Used by permission.

Extract p. 88 taken from the song "Jesus You Are Changing Me" by Marilyn Baker, copyright © 1981 Authentic Publishing/Adm. by Integrity Music, part of the David C Cook family, songs@integritymusic.com

Unless otherwise indicated, Scripture quotations are taken from the Holy Bible, New International Version Anglicised. Copyright © 1979, 1984, 2011 Biblica, formerly International Bible Society. Used by permission of Hodder & Stoughton Ltd, an Hachette UK company. All rights reserved. "NIV" is a registered trademark of Biblica. UK trademark number 1448790.

Scripture quotations marked "The Message" taken from The Message. Copyright © by Eugene H. Peterson 1993, 1994, 1995, 1996, 2000, 2001, 2002.Used by permission of NavPress Publishing Group.

Scripture quotations marked "NKJV" taken from the New King James Version. Copyright © 1982 by Thomas Nelson, Inc. Used by permission. All right reserved.

Scripture quotations marked "AMP" taken from the Amplified® Bible, Copyright © 1954, 1958, 1962, 1965, 1987 by The Lockman Foundation. Used by permission.

Scripture quotations marked "NLT" taken from the Holy Bible, New Living Translation, copyright © 1996, 2004, 2007 by Tyndale House Foundation. Used by permission of Tyndale House Publishers, Inc., Carol Stream, Illinois 60188. All rights reserved.

Scripture quotations marked "GNB" taken from the Good News Bible © 1994 published by the Bible Societies/HarperCollins Publishers Ltd UK, Good News Bible© American Bible Society 1966, 1971, 1976, 1992. Used with permission.

Scripture quotations marked "NJB" taken from The New Jerusalem Bible, published and copyright © 1985 by Darton, Longman and Todd Ltd and Doubleday, a division of Random House, Inc.

Picture credits:
Bill Bain: pp. 56, 58, 78; Alan Bedding: pp. 11, 20; Roger Chouler: pp. 2, 3, 24, 32, 62, 67, 91, 94; Getty: p. 80 © Stanislav Pobytov/Getty; Alison Hickey: pp. 42, 44; iStock: p. 9 © RASimon/iStockphoto. com, p. 17 © texelart/istockphoto.com, p. 25 © roballen38/iStockphoto.com, p. 28 © shalamov/iStockphoto.com, p. 33 © Alina Solovyova-Vincent/iStockphoto. com, p. 40 © Marek Mnich/iStockphoto. com, p. 41 © vid64/iStockphoto.com, p. 75 © kevron2001/iStockphoto.com, p. 87 © Pontuse/iStockphoto.com, p. 88 © rudisill/ iStockphoto.com; Len Kerswill: pp. 13, 26, 37, 76, 82; Estelle Lobban, pp. 14, 15, 18, 19, 21, 23, 24, 29, 31, 34, 37, 38, 43, 47, 50, 51, 56, 60, 63, 65, 68, 73, 79, 85, 90; Jonathan Roberts: p. 35; Anne Rogers: pp. 38, 47, 73; Debbie Willer: pp. 49, 53–54, 71